Joey's Journey
Saving Joey
A True Life Story

By Joseph K. Wood
Illustrated by Theresa Cates

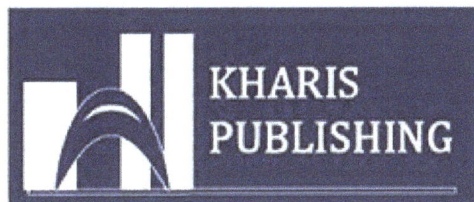

KHARIS PUBLISHING

All KHARIS PUBLISHING products are available at special quantity discounts for bulk purchase for sales promotions, premiums, fund-raising, and educational needs.

For details, write:
Kharis Media LLC
709 SW Elmside Drive
Bentonville, AR 72712

Tel: 1-479-599-8657
info@kharispublishing.com
www.kharispublishing.com

Saving Joey

A True Life Story

The young mother sat on her bed and sobbed. She just had a beautiful brown-eyed baby boy. Although thrilled to have a baby, she is sad that she cannot provide a good life for her baby. Tears of joy and sorrow flowed together.

She wrapped the baby in sheets and a soft blanket from her bed and laid him in an old basket she found in her closet. It was extremely cold in Chicago, and she wanted the tiny baby boy to be safe.

The determined young girl bundled herself up too and carried the baby into the night. So cold! So scared!

"Here! I will leave you here," she whispered when she got to an apartment building just a few blocks from her home, the cold air and tears freezing on her face.

The baby wiggled under the warm blanket but remained quiet.

She tucked the basket on the doorsteps of the apartment building, out of the falling snow.

"May you be safe, my precious baby!" she prayed as the snow flurries blew in the night.

She ran across the street and watched the basket on the steps from behind a tree. She hoped it would not be long before her baby boy would be okay.

Suddenly, a light shone
above the door. A soldier
named Ceaser opened
the door and walked down
the stairs. He stopped. He
noticed the wooden basket!

The blanket in the basket moved. Ceaser then lifted a corner of the blanket. He looked closer and saw a baby crying under the soft blanket.

"It's okay!" he told the baby. "Shhhh! Shhhh! Come on! It's okay!"

But the baby boy kept on crying.

Ceaser didn't know what to do. He looked around. He looked up and down the street but saw no one. Then he looked back down at the crying baby.

"Shhhh!" he said. "It's okay. Let's get you inside where it's warm!"

There was a note: 'Please take care of my baby, Joey!"

Ceaser picked up the basket, careful not to slip on the ice. He rushed the baby into the warmth of the apartment building.

"Sweetheart, there's a baby on the front steps!" Ceaser called to his wife.

The young girl behind the tree watched the man take her baby inside the apartment building. She waited a little while longer, sniffling quietly. Then she returned home.

"Sweetheart, where are you? I found a b-a-b-y outside on the stairs!" Ceaser called.

Finally, his wife appeared. Together, Ceaser and his wife pulled back the blanket.

They looked at each other. At that moment, Joey cried.

Ceaser called a few of his neighbors to come and help.

"What is going on, Ceaser?" asked a neighbor.

"Whose baby is this?" another neighbor asked.

"Is the baby hungry?"

"Was he outside in the snow and ice?"

Time passed very quickly. The apartment was busy with neighbors, all wanting to help. Joey had quieted down. He was safe and warm inside.

Ceaser called the police to come. The police officers asked Ceaser and the neighbors questions. They also checked the neighborhood for any clues as to who might have left the baby out in the cold weather, but they didn't find the mother.

So they returned to Ceaser and his wife and their apartment full of neighbors— and to Joey, asleep now in a neighbor woman's arms.

Ceaser and the police officers thanked the neighbors for coming to help. They wrapped Joey back up in his blanket and tucked him back in the basket.

One police officer told Ceaser, "You saved this little boy. I know you were surprised, but you did a good thing tonight!"

Ceaser and his wife kissed the little baby goodbye. The police left the apartment building with Joey. They took him to St. Vincent's Orphanage downtown.

Ceaser and his wife talked about what happened all night. Joey would be safe in the orphanage. They were thankful to be a part of saving Joey's life.

About the Author:

Joseph K. Wood, a foundling. Abandoned as a newborn on the streets of Chicago, he would later be adopted from St. Vincent's Orphanage. Joseph became a teen leader in the tough neighborhood of Jeffery Manor. Since then he has grown and has held key leadership positions as a bank examiner with Illinois Commissioner of Banks, assistant director with the University of Chicago Booth School, head of recruitment at Walmart International and Deputy Secretary of State for the Arkansas Secretary of State Office. Joseph Wood is an elected official and currently serves in Arkansas as the Washington County Judge.

Wood is the author of two children's books, Saving Joey and Adopting Joey (Joey's Journey Series). He has written the forewords of two nonfiction books and he is currently writing his autobiography. He is also a 2017 Angels in Adoption honoree, recognized by the Congressional Coalition on Adoption (CCAI). The CCAI raises awareness about orphans and foster children in need of loving familes.

Joseph lives in Fayetteville, Arkansas, with his wife June, daughters, and mother-in-law.
Go to the website, www.joeysjourneyseries.org, and sign up to be notified for upcoming releases and/or to book Joseph for a reading or lecture or to speak to your group, church, or business. Book reading and painting workshops are available for youths and adults with Joseph and Theresa Cates.

About the Illustrator:

Theresa Cates is native Arkansan. She started painting as a youth and found it was a necessary expression she could share with others. Theresa Cates may be reached at www.majesticmotions.com.

RESOURCES FOR FOSTER CARE, ADOPTION AND FAMILY

Family Council
www.familycouncil.org

Loving Choices
www.lovingchoices.org

The Call
www.thecallinarkansas.org

Arkansas Right to Life
www.artl.org

Compassion House
www.compassionhouse.us

Congressional Coalition on Adoption
www.ccainstitute.org/

ABOUT KHARIS PUBLISHING

Kharis Kids is an imprint of Kharis Publishing. Kharis Publishing is a traditional publishing house with a core mission to establish mini-libraries or resource centers for orphanages in developing countries, so these kids will learn to read, dream, and grow. A portion of the proceeds from books go towards establishing these resource centers. Every time you purchase a book from Kharis Publishing or partner as an author, you are helping give these kids an amazing opportunity to read, dream, and grow. Learn more at www.kharispublishing.com.

www.ingramcontent.com/pod-product-compliance
Lightning Source LLC
Chambersburg PA
CBHW050641150426
42813CB00054B/1150